Digital Detox
Rediscovering Balance in a Sustainable and Mindful Life

Table of Contents

Chapter 1. Introduction

In our special report, "Digital Detox: Rediscovering Balance in a Sustainable and Mindful Life," we embark on a jubilant journey, truly a navigational guide for anyone seeking equilibrium amidst our ever-connected world's cacophony. This report is not so much technical literature as it is a lantern, casting a warm, enlightening glow over a path less traveled, yet immensely rewarding. Within these pages lies a treasure trove of practical strategies and accessible wisdom designed to inspire, invigorate, and ultimately transform your relationship with technology. Navigating this digital seascape, this report invites you to embrace the notion that, indeed, less can be infinitely more. Let's laugh together, let's learn together, let's pursue the promise of a more sustainable, mindful life - free from the shackles of digital overload. If happiness and harmony are what you seek, rest assured: you don't need to look any further! Secure your copy today and embark on an adventure that promises to renew your zest for life.

Chapter 2. The Digital Quagmire: Understanding the Issue

Imagine a world where you wake up each morning, not to the soulful refrains of songbirds, but to the insistent pinging of your smartphone. Instead of reaching for a steaming cup of aromatic coffee or having a quiet, introspective moment to greet the day, your hand automatically extends towards your digital device, the umbilical cord of digital life. Does it sound familiar? You're not alone. This is the digital quagmire.

2.1. Entangled in the Web of Connectivity

Once a luxury, digital devices are now our constant companions, intertwined inextricably with our lives. Or should we say, we are intertwined inextricably within their invisible digital webs. We live in a world where the boundaries between online and offline are blurred, where people's worth is often measured not by their character traits but by their online profiles, where human connections are frequently made and measured in digital terms.

We've deep-dived into digital life, immersing ourselves in tweetstorms and Facebook updates, engaging in endless discussions in chat rooms, exploring YouTube rabbit holes, and bouncing between apps like ping pong balls. So much so that we've lost sight of time, of reality, of the essence of human interaction, and indeed, of ourselves.

Experts argue that this dependence on connectivity changes our cognitive functions. Our minds are always alert, always anticipating the next tweet, the next comment, the next interaction. It's addictive and exhaustive, leaving little room for tranquillity or introspection.

2.2. The Fallouts of Digital Addiction

Evidence indicates that excessive connectivity is linked with several negative outcomes, including increased anxiety and depression. One study found that teenagers who spend seven hours or more on screens are more than twice as likely to be diagnosed with depression or anxiety than those who use screens for an hour a day. Even adults are not immune.

This digital obsession is also associated with sleep issues. The harsh light of screens interferes with our circadian rhythms, making a restful night's sleep elusive. Moreover, the engaging nature of content leaves us scrolling late into the night, delaying sleep unnecessarily.

2.3. Reconnecting with the Disconnect

Despite the fallouts, it's critical to understand that our objective is not to villainize technology. On the contrary, technology and digital devices play a colossal role in our lives, providing information, entertainment, connectivity, and convenience at unprecedented levels. They have changed the way we work, learn, communicate, and even meet our basic needs. The problem lies not with the technology itself but with our relationship with it.

So the question stands - How do we leverage the power of technology without succumbing to its pitfalls? How do we improve our digital habits for a more balanced, mindful life?

2.4. The Science of Habits

Drawing from research in psychology, a habit forms when an action becomes automatic, typically after repeated performance in stable contexts. In the case of digital devices, the ease of access and engagement leads to recurrent use, quickly leading to habitual usage.

It might be daunting, but habits can certainly be broken, or better yet, replaced with healthier behaviors.

2.5. Road to Digital Detoxification

The journey to digital detoxification is not a sprint but a marathon. It's a process of replacing unhealthy digital habits with more mindful, healthier behaviors. It begins with small, doable steps, like setting screen time limits or creating device-free zones at home.

Next, consider periodically going offline. It could be a few hours each day or an entire day in the week - the idea is to disconnect digitally to reconnect with the physical world around you.

Sleep hygiene is another area where changes can substantially improve well-being. Making your bedroom a device-free zone can help you ease into a rhythm conducive to restful sleep.

Lastly, remember to take this quest gently, with kindness for yourself. Change is hard, and there will be setbacks. That's okay. As long as the general trend is towards healthier, more mindful digital behaviors, you're heading in the right direction.

Our exploration of the digital quagmire is by no means exhaustive, but we believe it's a good starting point in understanding, acknowledging, and eventually confronting our digital habits. The idea is not to eliminate digital devices from our lives completely but to strike a balance that allows us to lever their benefits without them taking over our lives. Because in the journey of life, we should be the ones charting our course, not our devices.

Chapter 3. Rewiring Our Minds: The Impact of Digital Overload

A surplus of stimuli meets our senses as the digital world unfolds through our screens, a ceaseless pulsing energy that increasingly controls our waking lives. As the digital age continues to evolve, it's imperative to examine the effects of this transformative shift on our mental health and overall wellbeing, with an emphasis on how to wield the power of technology mindfully.

3.1. A Torrent of Distraction

Our day begins, in most cases, with reaching for our phones, checking emails, and scrolling through social media feeds. The problem is, this undiluted dose of information as soon as we wake up floods our brains, putting us in a reactive mode from the beginning of the day. The digital overload not only impacts our productivity but also our mental health. Exposure to social media, the news, and endless streams of information makes the brain work overtime, limiting our ability to focus on individual tasks due to a phenomenon known as "cognitive load."

The mind, when inundated with more information than it can process, experiences cognitive overload. This circumstances influence our decision-making abilities and impede our learning engagement. Our attention spans become shorter as we juggle various information inputs, leading to what experts call "continuous partial attention."

3.2. Impact on Cognitive Development

The digital overload impacts not just our productivity but also our cognitive development and memory function. Every time we are unable to remember a simple fact or a beloved one's birthday, we are observing the impact of digital overload on our minds. Our dependency on search engines and digital tools to recall information is weakening our memory and may lead to digital dementia.

To settle our minds and regain control over our cognitive abilities, it's essential to strike a balance between our analog and digital lives. This would not just take the load off our minds but would also provide us the mental space to breathe, think, and grow.

3.3. Impact on Mental Health

Beyond cognition, digital overload can also influence our psychological health. Social media, a primary contributor to information overload, has been linked to anxiety, depression, and lower self-esteem. While it promises connection, an over-dependence on these platforms often leads to feelings of isolation and inadequacy due to a phenomenon termed the "comparison trap."

Taking regular breaks from the digital sphere and building meaningful connections in the physical world can help mitigate these adverse effects on mental health. It's more vital than ever to foster an environment in which mental health is prioritized, and the importance of mindfulness and presence is recognized.

3.4. Metamorphosis through Mindfulness

Practicing mindfulness, recognizing our digital consumption patterns, and setting boundaries for ourselves can tackle the problem of digital overload. Digital mindfulness is about regulating the usage of our digital devices consciously and purposefully, allowing us to reclaim our time, and with it, our peace of mind.

Incorporating basic practices such as a "digital detox" - refraining from using digital devices for a set period, can bring remarkable changes in our mood, focus, and overall well-being. Similarly, designating certain time slots for usage and non-usage during the day helps us to manage screen time better.

3.5. The Virtue of Balance

Developing resilience against the tide of information is a challenge we must learn to embrace. Achieving a balance doesn't mean eradication of technology; instead, it calls for a revised, mindful interaction. It is not about using less technology, but using technology less. A considered approach to balancing our digital and physical lives can help us work towards a healthier, much-needed equilibrium.

By discovering practices to efficiently handle digital distractions and overhaul our mindset towards technology, we can control the omnipresent information torrent. It's a journey that requires constant effort but promises to bring notable changes to our cognitive functions, mental health, and ultimately our lives. We evolve with technology, and it's time to make this evolution a conscious, mindful process.

Digital overload, due to its insidious nature, is a very real challenge in our increasingly connected world. However, by recognizing its impacts, we can take deliberate steps towards mitigating its effects and establishing a harmonious balance between our digital footprints and physical reality, heading towards sustainability for our minds and our path into the future.

Chapter 4. Creating Boundaries: Practical Steps to a Balanced Digital Life

Our lives today are intertwined with technology. Smartphones, tablets, computers; they each serve as conduits to an expansive digital world. While technology can foster connections, drive innovation, and create convenience, it can also become an overwhelming force if not appropriately managed. The key to balance is the creation of boundaries. By learning how to regulate our digital connections consciously, we can fully enjoy the useful tools of technology without succumbing to the cons of connectivity.

4.1. Understanding the Need for Digital Boundaries

Let's begin by understanding why digital boundaries are crucial. When we are incessantly plugged in, we lend credence to every email, notification, or message that comes our way. The incessant information can clutter our minds, distract our focus, and displace our precious time. In the rush of this digital downpour, our personal lives, wellness, and real-world relationships may suffer.

Acknowledge your personal limits. Are you snapping at family members after spending hours on work emails? Losing sleep thanks to the relentless dive into web-browsing, feeds, and threads? Start noting the impact of a boundary-less digital life and comprehend this indispensable need for regulating your digital habits.

4.2. The Triangle of Constraints: Time, Attention, Energy

Next, let's appreciate the Triangle of Constraints, comprising time, attention, and energy. Think of these assets as finite resources. Consider this: you have 24 hours a day, and part of it necessitates rest, leisure, meals, and other essential activities.

Every digital interaction comes at a cost against these constraints. When you spend hours binge-watching a series, you can't leverage the same hours for reading, exercising, or pursuing a hobby. It's a zero-sum game.

Paying heed to these constraints is a vital step toward creating effective digital boundaries.

4.3. Identifying Time-suckers: Audit Your Digital Use

To make effective changes, it is essential to first understand your current usage patterns. A variety of apps and software can lend itself to this cause. These digital tools will track your activity and online habits, providing a revealing insight into your usage patterns.

From such an audit, derive the essential and non-essential aspects of your digital use. Do you lose hours scrolling through social media feeds? Do incessant emails disrupt your focus during work? An honest audit will guide you to the necessary actions.

4.4. The Three D's: Delete, Delegate, Defer

To begin creating digital boundaries, we need to make conscious choices. Approach your digital usage with the three D's: Delete, Delegate, and Defer.

'Delete' signifies removing unnecessary apps or limiting mindless browsing. For instance, do you truly need that game on your phone, or can you substitute it for an engaging novel?

'Delegate' embraces the fact that you don't have to bear the entire digital burden yourself. Can you assign email screenings or data entry tasks to another team member?

'Defer' implies scheduling specific times for digital tasks. Instead of constant monitoring, can you designate two particular slots in a day to check and respond to emails?

This triage of your digital life will not only allow you more control but also ensure purposeful use of your digital commodities.

4.5. Setting up a Digital Detox Schedule

A Digital Detox Schedule serves as your manual for incorporating breaks from the digital world. These periods can range from a few minutes to days, or even weeks. The objective is to disengage temporarily from the digital realm and reconnect with your natural surroundings.

In these moments of digital pause, you might choose to meditate, read, exercise, or simply reflect in solitude. You could also cultivate 'Tech-free Zones' at home, such as dinner tables and bedrooms, where digital devices are strictly off-limits.

4.6. Unplugging from Work Post Official Hours

Work boundaries are especially important in this age of remote work and global colleagues. Come to an understanding with your team about digital communication outside of working hours unless in case of an urgent situation.

Switching off notifications or setting them to 'Do Not Disturb' mode post your 'official' work hours can help enforce this boundary. It not only helps you unwind and detach from the worries of work but also adds to a healthy work-life balance.

4.7. Using 'Airplane mode' More Often

Airplane mode is not just for flights anymore. By activating this feature in specific time-blocks or situations, you can nip distractions in the bud. It's incredibly effective when you need to focus on an intensive task or when you're about to engage in restful activities like reading or sleeping.

By creating digital boundaries, we can make technology work for us, not against us. Initially, it may be a challenge to disconnect. Yet, with discipline, persistence, and a clear understanding of the 'why,' the transformation of your digital life can lead to profound changes in your overall wellbeing. Begin your journey of techno-self awareness and discernment. Discover the richness of mindfully measured digital involvement and the resulting amplified human experience. Embrace the wisdom of knowing when to switch 'on' and when to switch 'off.' The power is in your hands.

Chapter 5. Mindfulness in a Digital Age: The Art and Science

In the grand tapestry of human existence, our technology-infused era presents an intoxicating blend of opportunities and challenges. On the one hand, technology has lovingly served as our society's lifeline, as a resounding beacon of progress and connectivity. Conversely, it has equally woven a maze of distractions, stressors, and disconnect that can leave us feeling lost and depleted.

Seeking balance amidst this noisy symphony of pings, pop-ups, and notifications is an art in itself. It is here that we call upon the ancient wisdom of mindfulness, a practice that allows us to cultivate awareness and presence amidst the whirlwind of our daily lives. It's time we explored the interplay of this age-old wisdom with our digital age—an encounter that, in fact, has tremendous potential to help us find grounding in our increasingly online existence.

5.1. The Science of Mindfulness

You need not delve deep into the world of mindfulness before you tumble upon its scientific underpinnings. The potent blend of psychology, neuroscience, and human behavior renders mindfulness not just a mystical ideology, but a well-researched, objectively beneficial practice.

Modern studies in mindfulness reveal its capability to alter brain patterns, leading to real physiological changes. These alterations pave the way for enhanced focus, improved emotional regulation, and boosted resilience—precisely what we need to traverse the digital landscape unscathed.

Amongst the regions of the brain affected, the prefrontal cortex—responsible for executive functions like decision making and self-control—shows increased activity during mindfulness practices. This development encourages a thoughtful, less reactive engagement with technology and the incessant information it presents.

5.2. The Art of Mindfulness in Combatting Digital Fatigue

Mindfulness in the technological context is as much an art as it is a science. It's about observing your relationship with your devices, your reactions and emotions to notifications, and your online habits without judgment.

As intricate as a dance, you'll learn to foster healthier digital interactions, developing an intuitive rhythm that respects your mental and emotional limits. For instance, reflexively scrolling through news feeds can be countered with 'tech breaks,' where you intentionally step away from devices and repurpose that time for self-reflection or connection with your physical surroundings.

To learn this dance, however, we must start from the foundation—bringing mindfulness into our daily interactions with technology. Starting with observing and becoming fully present in our technological routines can provide insights into psychological patterns that often go unnoticed. This practice illuminates the autopilot mode we often engage in while interacting with our digital devices.

5.3. Striving for a Mindful Tech-User Relationship

Achieving a new norm—a symbiotic relationship that honours both our digital realities and our human needs—requires active participation.

A purposeful integrative approach may involve setting designated zones inside your home where devices are not permitted, making bedtimes tech-free, or even incorporating regular digital detoxes. Such actions allow us to reclaim control from the incessant rhythm of notifications and updates.

Remember, it's not about renouncing technology but about developing a mindful relationship where our interaction with devices enhances our lives rather than dominates them. It's about rebalancing our scale to ensure our digital commitments do not encroach upon our personal joy, tranquility, or the quality of our 'offline' relationships.

5.4. Harnessing Technology to Facilitate Mindfulness

Ironically, while we strive to minimize our digital overloading, certain technological tools can assist us in embedding mindfulness into our lives.

Apps dedicated to meditation, mindfulness exercises, or mental health can serve as supportive allies in our quest for digital equilibrium. These digital helpers can provide means to step back, breathe, and regain our composure amid our bustling schedules. They can be our reminders to pause, pay attention, and tune into our inner state of being—powerful steps in fostering mindfulness.

This technological aid, coupled with personal efforts toward digital self-awareness, can be pivotal in crafting a balanced and sustainable digital life. Technology can thus be used as a springboard for mindfulness rather than a hindrance to it.

5.5. The Potential of Mindful Tech-Use for Future Generations

As we craft a mindful model of tech-use for ourselves, we are simultaneously shaping the landscape that the younger generation will inherit. With children's digital plugging-in age decreasing, it's more crucial than ever to ensure the digitally aware practices we develop are transferable and adaptable to them.

Children's intuitive ability to mimic patterns they observe warrants our commitment to practice what we advocate—mindful tech use. By personally modeling the appropriate interaction with technology—a balance of connectivity and disconnection—we teach the younger generation an approach to digital life that values personal wellbeing and genuine human connection.

5.6. Crafting Your Personal Path to Mindful Tech-Use

Every person's digital landscape is as unique as their fingerprint. Thus, there is no 'one-size-fits-all' strategy for developing mindful tech-use.

Identify digital habits or patterns that seem to deplete your energy or mood. Take note of how different platforms or uses affect you, both mentally and physically. Make gradual changes, prioritizing those areas that seem to impact you most significantly. Remember, the objective is not perfection but progression—growth in personal awareness, self-regulation, and, ultimately, balance.

With this guidance, you are well-equipped to begin navigating the intricate loop of mindfulness and technology. Each small action you take towards mindful tech use will be a monumental step in creating a digital landscape where technology serves you, not the other way around. And ultimately, into embracing a balanced, sustainable, and mindful life in our digital age.

Chapter 6. Detoxification: Safely Disconnecting from Digital Devices

The onslaught of digital devices, from smartphones to tablets, laptops to smartwatches, indeed, has brought convenience and efficiency to our lives. Yet, they also bring with them a constant barrage of notifications, updates, and distractions that can overwhelm our senses and hijack our time. The need for a safe and mindful disconnection from these digital dependencies has perhaps never been greater than now.

6.1. The Need for Detoxification

We're inundated daily with myriad forms of digital information – text messages, emails, social media notifications, work announcements, news alerts, all vying for our attention and encroaching upon our already limited time. This ongoing distraction wreaks havoc on our minds, affecting sleep patterns, reducing concentration, fostering stress, and impacting mental health. Digital detoxification is not about completely eliminating technology from our lives, but rather about striking a judicious balance, fostering healthier habits that enable positive engagement with our devices.

6.2. Understanding the Effects of Digital Overload

To comprehend the deepest need for this digital detoxification, it's integral to discern the potential harm brought about by digital overload. This involves psychological impacts such as increased anxiety and depression, alongside physical manifestations such as impaired vision and disrupted circadian rhythms. Studies indicate that excessive screen time can lead to health issues like heart disease, obesity, and diabetes. Furthermore, digital overload can disrupt personal relationships, work productivity, and overall life satisfaction.

6.3. Taming the Mind: The First Step Towards Digital Detox

The first step towards digital detoxification is pausing to observe our relationship with our devices. Are we using technology as a tool, or is it beginning to control our life? Developing mindfulness about our digital consumption can help us perceive patterns that may be detrimental to our wellbeing. Implementing mindfulness techniques, such as meditation, deep breathing, and journaling, paves the way for greater self-awareness, leading towards the path of balance and control.

6.4. Practical Strategies for Digital Detoxification

Once we have identified the issue and acknowledged the need for detoxification, the next step moves towards practical strategies that encourage a healthier digital diet.

1. **Creating Tech-Free Zones**: Designate specific areas in your home as tech-free zones. This could be your bedroom, dining room, or any place that you associate with relaxation or quality time with family.

2. **Setting Clear Boundaries**: Allocate specific hours of the day as 'electronics-free' time. This might be during meals, an hour before bed, or first thing in the morning.

3. **Smartphone Detox**: Minimize the use of smartphones. Uninstall

unnecessary apps, turn off notifications for non-essential functions, and limit screen time with built-in features or third-party applications.

4. **Engaging in Offline Activities**: Pursue hobbies that don't involve digital devices. Reading physical books, gardening, painting, or any recreational activities that demand physical presence can serve as effective substitutes.

5. **Digital Detox Retreats**: If you need a more drastic step, consider digital detox retreats. These specialized getaways involve a complete disconnection from technology, and provide strategies to handle digital overload in your daily life.

6.5. Staying Committed to the Digital Detox Journey

Embracing the digital detox journey invariably requires a level of commitment and discipline. You may face difficulties, especially during the initial period. But remember, this is a step towards well-being. Keep a journal for noting your progress, share your journey with your loved ones for support, and most importantly, celebrate little victories.

6.6. Redefining Relationship with Digital Devices

Approaching technology mindfully doesn't mean completely renouncing digital devices. Instead, it implores us to define boundaries, bringing intention to our digital interactions. Technology, when used judiciously, can prove to be an effective tool for productivity, learning, communication and entertainment.

In conclusion, digital detoxification is a calibrated process – a bridge that leads us from an impulsive, addictive relationship with our devices to a more mindful, balanced interface. Remember, the road to digital detox is not always easy, and there could be times when you may veer off the path. But, every step you take towards reducing your digital footprint, no matter how small, lights your way towards a healthier, more balanced lifestyle, fundamentally transforming your relationship with technology. So embark on this journey today, and discover a new, refreshing perspective towards leading a sustainable and mindful life.

Chapter 7. Analog Echoes: Embracing Physicality in a Digital Era

The digital age, while brimming with opportunities, can at times feel like an overbearing entity seeping into every corner of our existence. With the glimmering allure of convenience and connectivity, it is easy to forget the charm of an older, tactile existence, a life embraced in the heart of analog experiences.

7.1. Nostalgia of the Tangible

Amidst screens and touch interfaces, we've lost the warmth of letterpress typography, the ambience of vinyl records, the charm of handwritten letters, or the feel of physical books. So, yet, they hold a certain magic that is amiss in their digital duplications: a 'touch-feel' interface that remains unchallenged. There's an undeniable authenticity when you hold a physical object, an immediate connection that goes beyond just senses. It is an experience both simple, yet extraordinary, as though we're touching a piece of the past, yet remaining completely in the present. A fusion of nostalgia and now.

7.2. Re-embracing Analog Values

Transforming our relationship with technology not only requires a conscious effort to become less dependent on our devices, but also means rediscovering and embracing the analog characteristics we've been missing out on. This process doesn't just involve turning off digital devices, but actively replacing them with rewarding analog activities.

For instance, instead of relying on your smartphone to remind you of important dates, how about re-embracing the wall calendar? Or perhaps replacing some of your online reading time with borrowing books from your local library? These are simple yet profound shifts which serve to re-anchor ourselves in the physical world. They are echoes from the analog era that have not only sustained but also become more relevant with time.

7.3. Committing to Physicality

Bringing back physicality into our lives can also unearth immense potential for creativity and sensory development that digital interfaces cannot wholly capture. Analog activities like painting, cooking, playing musical instruments, or even the forgotten joy of handwriting are pursuits that require our full engagement- mentally and physically. These activities can serve as meditative practices that enhance focus and mindfulness, detaching us from the digital rush and immersing us in the 'now'.

At the heart of committing to physicality is adapting the concept of 'Slow Living'- a lifestyle emphasizing slower approaches to aspects of everyday life. It suggests focusing on quality over quantity, valuing the time spent in each activity, and giving full attention to the task at hand. In essence, it's about going back to the basics and embracing them fully.

7.4. Practical Ways to Reembrace Analog in Daily Life

The idea of completely disconnecting might seem daunting. However, introducing analog components into your life doesn't have to be an abrupt, all-or-nothing shift.

- **Digital Sunset**: Designate a certain time each evening when you will disconnect from all digital devices. During this time, engage in non-digital activities that you enjoy.

- **Write It Down**: Swap your smartphone notes for a traditional notebook. Capture ideas, plan your day, or just doodle on physical paper.

- **Read Real Books**: Instead of downloading another eBook, consider visiting your nearest library or bookstore and finding a physical book to read.

- **Get in touch with nature**: Take a walk, go hiking, or simply sit in a park. Connect with the real world around you.

- **Meet face-to-face**: While video calls and chats have their place, make an effort to gather with friends and loved ones in person when possible.

- **Cook your meals**: Take a break from food delivery apps and cook a meal. Engage with senses in selecting, preparing and consuming food.

- **Art and Craft**: Engage in activities like painting, knitting, gardening for mindfulness, creativity, and therapeutic care.

7.5. Acknowledging the Partnership: Analog and Digital

As we invite more analog experiences into our lives, it's essential to understand that this isn't a battle between analog and digital, but rather a harmonious symbiosis that we're aiming to achieve. Digital technology and analog experiences can play together beautifully if calibrated correctly. Digital tools can provide unbounded opportunities for connection, learning, and creation, and analog activities can ground us, bring us closer to our senses, and add depth to our human experiences.

One doesn't supersede the other, but, like yin and yang, they balance each other out. The ultimate goal is to develop a mindful, sustainable existence that honors both the digital and analog aspects of our lives. In emphasizing quality engagement, experiences, and mindful living, we get to bring out the best of both worlds.

After all, balance is not achieved by completely eliminating one aspect but by learning to navigate and integrate both effectively into our lives. One thing is for sure, too much of anything is never good, and the best way forward is always through balance, moderation, and the timeless wisdom of 'less is more'.+

Now that you've embarked on this journey, remember the importance of patience and grace with yourself. Changes take time, especially when they're profound and worthwhile! Enjoy the process, and take comfort in knowing that every small step you take towards embracing analog and physicality in your life is paving the way for larger transformations.

Remember, every echo has a source and every source, a purpose. So, let's embrace these analog echoes and create a purposeful, balanced life filled with vibrancy, creativity, and peace.

Chapter 8. Implementing the Detox: A Practical Guide to Action

A pivotal turning point towards a balanced, sustainable and ultimately, happier life, is the implementation of a digital detox. This is the moment when theory and aspiration metamorphose into concrete action.

8.1. The Importance of Intent

Before you can immerse yourself in the bracing, liberating waters of digital detox, you must understand why you're taking the plunge in the first place. Start by asking yourself the following questions:

1. Why do I want to detox from digital devices?

2. How are these devices affecting my mental and physical health?

3. How do these devices affect my relationships?

4. What changes do I expect to see after my digital detox?

By seeking answers to these questions, you engage in an inner dialogue that can potentially yield interesting insights about your bond with technology.

8.2. Formulating a Personalized Digital Detox Plan

Having established your intent, it's time to draft a plan. Successful detox requires more than just a blunt cessation of device use; like any meaningful transformation, it demands thoughtful planning and strategic goal setting.

Your plan should be tailored to your individual needs, lifestyle, and desired outcomes, and it should cover:

1. The length of your detox – will it be a day-long cleanse, or a week-long reboot?

2. The specific devices or applications you aim to distance yourself from.

3. How will you account for work or other necessary digital interactions?

4. If you're seeking to break a specific habit, what alternatives will you use instead?

Use the information gleaned from your intent examination, combining it with practical considerations, to carefully craft a detox plan that is both achievable and beneficial.

1. Define the purpose of your digital detox

2. The duration of the detox period

3. Identify the "problematic" digital devices or applications

4. Tailor a replacement strategy

8.3. Stepping into Reality: Putting Plan into Action

Once you have your personalized plan, it's time to implement it. This phase can be challenging, as you're not only breaking away from a comfort zone, but also forging a new pathway in your daily life. Nevertheless, embracing this discomfort is crucial, as it catalyzes personal growth.

Here are some strategies for successful implementation:

1. Establish regular technology-free zones or periods.

2. Replace digital activities with analogue ones, like reading a physical book, going for a walk, or engaging in a hobby.

3. Utilize tools that can restrict access to certain websites or applications during designated periods. Several free and paid digital detox apps are available.

4. Communicate openly about your detox to those around you, so that they understand and support your cause.

It's important to remember two things:

1. You're bound to face temptation and possible slip-ups. However, rather than viewing these as failures, embrace them as learning opportunities.

2. Keep reassessing and adjusting your plan based on your experiences and feedback; aiming for perfection is less valuable than aiming for progress.

8.4. Nurturing Your Well-being

Digital detox is not an end in itself; rather, it's a mechanism to enhance your overall well-being. Hence, conscientiously integrating practices that rejuvenate your physical, mental and emotional health alongside your detox can be monumental in making the transition smoother and more fruitful.

Consequently, couple your detox with practices like mindful meditation, regular physical activity, maintaining a healthy diet, and prioritizing restful sleep.

Furthermore, regularly engaging in reflective practices, such as journaling, can provide surprising insights into your evolving relationship with technology and yourself.

8.5. Looking Beyond the Detox: Forming Sustainable Habits

Implementing your digital detox is an important step, but it is just the beginning. You've experienced a different way of living, one less dominated by the constant pings and notifications of digital life. The next step is ensuring this is not a mere flash in the pan, but a sustainable, long-term shift.

For this, consider the following:

1. Gradually adapt certain facets of your detox as permanent lifestyle changes; for instance, always maintaining a certain period of the day as tech-free.

2. Fostering a mindful approach to technology use, by being conscious of, and intentional about when and why you use digital devices.

3. Regularly self-assess your relationship with technology, tuning it as necessary to ensure balance and sustainability.

4. Share your journey and insights with others, inspiring them and creating a supportive community that values mindful technology use.

The path to a mindful, sustainable life free from digital overload may seem daunting. But by embracing change, confronting difficulties, and persisting on the path less traveled, you're embarking on a journey to a happier, more harmonious existence. Won't you take the first step today?

Chapter 9. Persistence and Consistency: Keeping up with your Digital Detox

Our journey begins with the two cornerstone principles that form the bedrock of a successful digital detox: Persistence and Consistency. The perfect harmony of these two powerful virtues can form a potent recipe for reclaiming control of your life from digital conundrum.

9.1. Understanding Persistence

At its core, persistence is an inherently human quality – an unyielding resolve that enables us to push through obstacles, however formidable they may be. In the context of a digital detox, persistence is the engine that fuels your ongoing commitment to free yourself from the shackles of digital overload.

A digital detox is not a one-time "switching off" process, but rather a continuing effort towards achieving balance between our lives online and offline. Persistence in this setting means pushing against the pervasive current of digital distractions and forging your own path towards greater tranquility.

However, persistence alone is not enough. Like all endeavors, there will be times when the sirens of our screens prove too compelling, luring us back into the clutches of the digital deluge. But remember, a single detour does not equate to an ultimate destination. Do not view these moments as failures, but rather as signposts on your journey, reminding you of the divergence between where you are and where you want to be. Each moment of challenge is an opportunity to reassert your steadfastness, underscoring the importance of your goal and breathing fresh life into your digital detox journey.

9.2. Nurturing Consistency

While persistence forms the intent, consistency forms the action. The true power of a consistent effort should never be underestimated. Just as a river, through countless years of unwavering flow, can carve valleys through solid rock, so too can a steady and consistent approach make lasting changes in your life.

Consistency in a digital detox means regularly committing to periods of disconnection, regardless of the chaos or demands that may confront you. It is the deliberate practice of creating and maintaining new habits that allow you to decompress, unwind, and redirect your attention towards the analog aspects of life that truly matter.

This could manifest as steadfast rules governing screen time, specific windows of digital disconnect every day, or weekend-long abstentions from all forms of digital media. These steady, small steps, performed with stalwart resolution, can form the steps leading to a life that is no longer mastered by digital encumbrances, but one that masters them.

To illustrate this, picture a garden filled with stones. Each stone represents a digital distraction or a habit that keeps you chained to your screens. Persistent efforts will give you the strength to move these stones, while consistent efforts will ensure you are tending your garden every day, preventing these stones from piling up again.

9.3. Practical Methods to Fuel Persistence and Consistency

Charging ahead without a roadmap can be a daunting endeavor. Here, we present a series of actionable steps to guide your journey towards achieving persistence and consistency.

1. Define Clear, Realistic Goals: Set achievable goals to inspire

commitment and determination. These act as your lighthouse guiding your ship through the turbulent seas of distractions.

2. Create a Routine: A specific routine helps to create familiarity, which in turn cultivates consistency. Allocate set times for digital activities, breaks, and complete digital disconnection.

3. Leverage Support Networks: Embarking on a journey is made easier with companions. Seek the support of family and friends. Share your commitment and progress with them and seek their understanding when you choose to be offline.

4. Practice Mindfulness: Mindful practices such as meditation and deep-breathing exercises not only serve as a respite from screens, but also enhance focus and determination.

5. Celebrate Your Achievements: Rewarding yourself for milestones achieved will further stoke the fires of your determination while acting as a reassurance of your progress.

6. Embrace Failures: Unable to resist a late-night scroll? Don't worry. Persistence is much about learning from failures as it is about relentless forward motion. Forgive yourself and bounce back.

In closing, a successful digital detox is a harmonious symphony of persistence and consistency: The rhythm of willpower strumming the chords of action, to play the captivating melody of digital freedom and peace. Take it one note, one beat at a time. The proverbial orchestra of digital euphony awaits you. So take up your baton and orchestrate a life where digital devices are tools for enhancement, not chains of enslavement. Are you ready for the crescendo?

Chapter 10. Case Studies: Real-Life Stories of Successful Digital Detox

There exists an intriguing spectrum of extraordinary stories, painting an inspiring picture of those who dared to press pause on digital distractions and succeeded in reclaiming their reality.

10.1. The Social Media Mogul

First in line, we have James, a 30-year-old social media mogul. From the moment he opened his eyes each day, a flurry of notifications plaguing his smartphone demanded his attention. Paired with the temptation to incessantly scroll, double-tap, and swipe, he found himself treading upon a path of digital dependency. It began infringing upon his real-life interactions and personal peace, awakening him to the necessity of a change.

James started with a simple action plan which consisted of refraining from using his phone during meals and social gatherings. Transiting from the screen to the warmth of face-to-face conversations was challenging yet rejuvenating. Instead of circulating updates about his experiences, he learnt to live each second of them mindfully. Gradually, FOMO (Fear Of Missing Out) diminished to a distant echo, failing to sway him.

After embracing this digital detox journey, James found himself consumed by a newfound serenity. His productivity rocketed, creativity no longer confined by virtually endorsed trends. A recent study comparing pre-and-post detox results affirmed his improvement, showing a decrease in digital usage by 40% accompanied by an equivalent increase in emotional well-being. His story serves as a testament to the power of self-control and the benefits of digital moderation.

10.2. The Tech-Reliant Teenager

Moving on, let's delve into the story of Sophia, a 16-year-old girl living in the digital age. As a teenager, her existence was largely influenced by the virtual world. Online schooling, video games, social media discourses - her life seemed enmeshed with technology. Yet the constant digital exposure took a toll on her mental health, rendering her anxious and sleep-deprived.

Sophia decided to conform to the 'Screen-Free Saturdays' concept, barring all forms of digital screens every Saturdays. It was an uphill battle at first, considering her reliance on digital devices. Yet, her perseverance saw her through the initial upheaval. She replaced digital recreation with offline hobbies such as painting, gardening and cycling in the park.

Sophia's decision to allocate time specifically for digital disconnect remarkably improved her mental health. Besides an evident uplift in her mood and concentration, she developed an enriching set of skills and hobbies. Sophia's experience underlines the potency of reserving tech-free time and the subsequent holistic health benefits.

10.3. The Entrepreneur Embracing Balance

Lastly, we spotlight Tom, a 50-year-old entrepreneur engrossed in the swirling world of start-ups. His love for technology and innovation was double-edged. While it facilitated his entrepreneurial pursuits, it disrupted his work-life balance, straining personal relationships and causing chronic stress.

His detox strategy was to designate device-free zones in his home and workspaces, leading to a reduction in stress and an increase in valuable interpersonal interactions. Additionally, Tom's commitment to regular 'off-screen' breaks throughout his workday reduced his perception of work-related stress and burnout. He began noticing patterns of stress build-up and effectively mitigated it by stepping away from the screen at regular intervals.

Tom's personal and professional life witnessed a significant transformation as he integrated digital detox practices into his daily ritual. Not only did he report a marked rise in productivity and efficiency, but his personal relationships also improved, painting a fulfilling image of work-life balance.

To conclude, these stories provide three distinct yet connected journeys of individuals from various walks of life. Though their digital detox routes may seem different, they share common attributes: perseverance, self-discipline, and resilience. Proof that detaching from digital dependence yields improvements to overall well-being, productivity and interpersonal relationships. Hence, the essence of these narratives lies in the potential they carry to inspire personal change towards a balanced digital lifestyle.

Chapter 11. The Afterglow: Flourishing in a Post-Detox Life

As our insightful journey through digital detoxification sums up, we find ourselves left with feelings both empty and euphoric - an unusual mix that marks the crux of our digital disconnect. The stage we term "The Afterglow." This phase isn't just about a newfound freedom from digital constraints; instead, it's about embracing the abundance of alternate possibilities that life extends and thriving amidst these choices.

11.1. The Beauty of Disconnection

The first thing you notice upon completing your digital detox is a profound sense of calmness. No incessant pings demanding your attention, no ceaseless scrolling, and no distractions. You'll find your days longer, your mind less cluttered, and your attention no longer divided.

But disconnecting from the digital world doesn't necessarily mean isolation. Quite the opposite: you're more present, more connected to those around you. You engage in deeper, more meaningful conversations, nurturing relationships that had been overshadowed by digital ones. And above all, you'll find yourself engaging with your environment on a much more profound level, observing the tiny details of nature and life that often escape our hurried, digital-driven gazes.

11.2. Cultivating Mindfulness

A crucial element to nurturing the afterglow of digital detox is mindfulness. Having divested from digital distractions, you now have the time to reflect inward, connect with your core, and observe your thoughts. This practice aids not just in self-awareness but also in mounting resilience against potential digital relapses.

To bolster your mindfulness, you can engage in basic meditation practices. Use your mornings or evenings - those times when you might have previously been engrossed in your devices - to sit in solitude and focus your mind. Practising mindfulness doesn't require much; think of it as simply being present in the moment without judgement.

11.3. Nurturing Real Relationships

We've mentioned how being disconnected digitally means being more connected physically, but it's crucial to underscore the significance that real-life connections hold for human vitality. Studies consistently find that individuals with strong social ties enjoy better mental and physical health, and even increased longevity.

Nurturing relationships in the post-detox world should be effortless, but it's good to be mindful and active about it. Make up for those lost moments by spending quality time with loved ones, actively participating in community events, or even reviving old neglected hobbies in the company of friends. Make every interaction count.

11.4. Reclaiming Time and Productivity

A significant benefit of digital detox is the abundance of time you'll reclaim. Where you were once entangled within the confines of digital consumption, you're now free to use these hours productively. Take this opportunity to invest time in professional development, personal growth, or recreational activities.

Moreover, the absence of constant digital interruptions allows for deeper focus and concentration, enabling better productivity. You'll find tasks that previously seemed arduous now breeze by because you're fully present and committed to them.

11.5. Designing a Healthy Digital Diet

While we advocate for a digital detox, we are by no means promoting a complete severance from digital life. After all, technology is a tool that, when used judiciously, enriches our lives and makes tasks more manageable.

Work towards a healthy digital diet, where you control when and how you engage with technology. This strategy might involve specific no-tech hours, designated email-checking times, or using apps with intention rather than mindless browsing. Balance is key in both the analog and digital domain.

In conclusion, flourishing in a post-detox life is not just about the absence of digital distractions but also about proactively engaging with the world with fresh, undistracted eyes. By claiming back time lost to scrolling, you gift yourself the room to breathe, to live, to connect, and to thrive - to experience life's afterglow in all its richness.